In book London, that will allow the child to enjoy this great capital without the expense or inconvenience of navigating the city in real life.

Colourful illustrations reveal the ever-improving landmarks that distinguish London from the otherwise uninteresting collection of people and places that make up the rest of our United Kingdom.

New words on each page emphasise the appeal of the city to the international elite, whose gracious investment in property serves to increase the material differences that keep us interesting.

Respectful appreciation of contemporary culture will help shake History from the historical in ways that avoid unneccesarily provoking the child or their imagination.

Dung Beetle is proud to offer this fabulously carbon-neutral, low-crime, risk-free alternative to leaving your home. Enjoy London as it is meant to be enjoyed: from the outside.

This book belongs to:

KEY SUBTEXTS is a new experimental
scheme exclusive to Dung Beetle Books, where
children are given stepping stones to the
interior meaning of a surface text. These come
in the form of three key words, each of which
give a clue to the authors' deeply sinister intent.
Eventually, your children will soon learn to
confuse insight with paranoia, and so develop
a  healthy, progressive outlook.

PALACE OF
WESTMINSTER

TATE MODERN

ST. PAUL'S
CATHEDRA

Book 2b

THE DUNG BEETLE NEW
WORDS READING SCHEME

# We see the

# sights

written and illustrated by
M.  ELIA & E. ELIA

Dung Beetle Ltd © 2022

DUNG BEETLE HQ

THE SHARD

Lockdown is over.

Now we will go on a tour of the town.

visiting        permit        granted

"Today is the anniversary of Amazon's conquest of everything, and this is the victory parade," says Mummy.

Kim Kardashian has replaced Lord Nelson.

"She has over three hundred million followers on social media," says Mummy.

There is a message for John on the big screen.

"Am I in trouble?" asks John.

"Yes," says Mummy. "Prepare for your public shaming."

The lion is wearing make up.

"He/she/they have truly joined the pride now, beams Mummy.

"That looks like a jolly fun ride," says John.

"It is watching you at all times," says Mummy.

.

"What is hate speech?"
asks John.

"Anything we hate,"
says Mummy.

new words    silent        padded        cell

We are at Parliament.

The MPs have been replaced with waxwork dummies.

"They are just as useful this way," says Mummy.

"Soon, we won't need any devices, because our bodies will merge with the system," chirps Mummy.

"I'm scared," says John.

"Why, what could possibly go wrong?" says Mummy.

.

new words    man    is    phone

Merge with your oyster card

We have decolonised the British Museum.

Now it is entirely empty.

"Can we go and see something else?" asks Jane.

The Cancel Culture
Drones are circling the
National Gallery.

"Run! They have detected
your  unconscious biases,
exclaims Mummy.

St Primark's Cathedral is now open for business.

"It is the spiritual cornerstone of our civilisation," says Mummy.

"We are in the Zero Emissions Zone," says Mummy.

"Please stop breathing till we leave."

"Why are those heads on sticks?" asks John.

"It is in the spirit of progress from our barbarous past," says Mummy.

We are at a souvenir shop.

"Here are the cheap totems of a dead empire," says Mummy.

Cupid has lost his bow and arrow.

"How are we supposed to fall in love now?" asks Susan.

"On Instagram, with ourselves," replies Mummy.

new words    loving        inward        attractio

There is one of the Queen's Gender-Queer Brigade.

"He looks just like my favourite ice lolly," says John.

new words    gender    fluid    lolly

We are throwing crypto in the fountain.

"Make a wish," says Mummy.

"I wish for real money," says Susan.

new words

intangible    wish    factory

"That's a big playground," says John.

"It is for the entertainmen of our financial overlords," says Mummy

"I don't want to go to the gallery," says Susan.

"Your cultural credit score are running low," says Mummy.

"If you don't go, you will have to walk home by yourself."

new words    cashless    punishment    system

## New words used in this book

| | |
|---|---|
| 6 visiting/ permit/ granted | 26 zero/ impact/ anywhere |
| 8 next-day/ delivery/ militia | 28 gentler/ headless/ society |
| 10 empty/ popularity/ contest | 30 loving/ inward/ attraction |
| 12 omniscient/ social/ credit | 32 gender/ fluid/ lolly |
| 14 merry/ pronoun/ potpourri | 34 intangible/ wish/ factory |
| 16 all/ seeing/ big wheel | 36 everything/ must/ go |
| 18 silent/ padded/ cell | 38 heavenly/ bargains/ galore |
| 20 melt/ down/ democracy | 40 big/ boy/ fruit-machines |
| 22 man/ is/ phone | 42 trinkets/ of/ doom |
| 24 insects/ of/ authority | 44 cashless/ payment/ system |

# Total number of new words 60

*Dedicated to the big mummy in the sky.*

First published 2022 © With thanks to Tania Edwards